I0606270

FROM AWAY

From Away

Eli Goldblatt

chax 2026

tucson arizona

ISBN: 978-1-946104-73-1

Chax Press / 6181 E 4th St / Tucson Arizona 85711 / USA

Chax Press books are supported in part by individual donors and by sales of books. Please visit *https://chax.org/membership-support/* if you would like to contribute to our mission to make an impact on the literature and culture of our time. Special thanks to Mary Ellen Bartholomew and André Spears for their generous and continuing support. Chax books have also been supported by the Arizona Commission on the Arts and the Arts Foundation for Tucson and Southern Arizona.

We thank our Art Director, Cynthia Miller, who contributes advice and support to all books Chax publishes.

The author thanks the following publications for publishing these poems:
"After the shooting," CCCC Convention Program, Pittsburgh 2019
"Gridded Window," *Wallace Stevens Journal*
"Adesso," *Hubbub*
"Sequestered," *Love and the Pandemic Anthology*, Moonstone Press
"Saylor's Grove," *Walkers in the City*, Ohm Editions anthology of Rain Taxi
"Side Streets," *Community Literacy Journal*
"Illusions clothe," *JWMM* Online
"Weathered Bench," *25th Anniversary Poetry Ink Anthology*, Moonstone Press

Wissahickon Creek: Walks & Dreams (Moonstone P, 2022) contained 30 pages of poems from the first two sections of this book. That chapbook was dedicated to Wissahickon Creek Park and the Friends of the Wissahickon, who care for this Philadelphia treasure.

Warm gratitude to the Corporation of Yaddo for a writing residence in November 2019.

Contents

To my brother
Aaron Goldblatt (1955-2025)
Advocate for Play

So, all particles in the universe are entangled.
Mei-Mei Berssenbrugge

Wherever I am, at whatever place on earth,
I hide from people the conviction that I'm not from here.
Czeslaw Milosz

. . . as if the image were the field which only just now,
in the dream, had once again been painfully ploughed,
and in which the seeds of my later life had then been sown.

Walter Benjamin

From Away

Inishmore

for JD

John, I thought of you when
I walked along miles of wall
piled in delicate tumult, gaps
for wind so you can see
cows & ocean thru heavy

lattice. One long rock scored
like window frames shelved
sideways in stone (I wonder, if
I drew them out, what panes
in rock might show), I took

photos but couldn't get
it right: my people left
no where with nothing—not
even a stone piled on stone.

Yorkshire Foot Path

curves up from the
flagstones across a cropped
meadow & beyond your red
raincoat in early morning
mist. My muscles resist the
hill's rise but rhythm carries
us till noon past black
faced Swaledale sheep
scattered over fells, staring
& chewing then running
a few feet away. Down
past waterfalls into Keld
tiny town with café serving
boiled eggs & muesli to
walkers from Denmark
Netherlands & London
chewing like village sheep.

Afternoon ahead, we turn
on the steep ascent when
wind picks up to see ruined
stone barns shadowing
stacked walls drawn to fit
wide grassy creases above
an invisible stream. We go
higher, view more abstract,
our jackets back on as we

reach the ridge. Near
evening, we enter enclosed
fields barely visible in fog.
Sheep—neither hurried nor
surprised—appear & dissolve
as we walk toward the next
narrow stile & back into
Muker with its old literary
center, bakery closed
today for a private funeral
& a carpark holding
Audis, Fiats & Fords.

After the shooting

answer email, pay a fine, invite
my brother to coffee tho I know
he won't be in town this week, clean
the upstairs toilet & sink, read a review
of a book about Western Australia
pet the cat.
                              All killings the same
in one sense: they leave a tear in
the cloth that can't be mended
or patched. Each death destroys
a world, the rabbis say, & a bell
rings in this hollow cavern I hear
again the same bell yet strange with
the passing of another traveler.

I can't do this. I can't write about
their deaths just because they could
be my aunt or cousins, dentist or
accountant, brother-in-law or friend.
History grows heinous when most
intimate & now the demons take me
by the chin, loving tug wrenches
my spine. I see light in the branches
outside my window, yellow leaves
almost ready to drop onto passive

soil gone dormant, & a spider's casual
trap for the slowing bee. You will
know the bell in your dreams, little

servant, you will break beneath dark
clods, the tone untainted by fear.

Everywhere else

Everywhere else I can stand & see
others walking away or toward me,
but here the street remains empty or
leads nowhere at all. The wind bends
tree limbs & I feel snow cut my cheek.
Traffic sounds at the edge of hearing
but no car comes into view. I look one
way or another but see nobody—no
birds in the moving branches, no open
sky beyond gray clouds. Perhaps I

haven't looked hard enough or the
neighborhood lies further from home
than I realized when I set out this
afternoon with little thought
for destination or companions.

Foreign Corridors

Among tomatoes & garlic from your garden,
we pour tea & make strained conversation.
You look down, not bewildered by our talk
but seeing instead sepia rooms your furious

brain frames, away from us. I want to make
you laugh or cry at memory of our two boys
doing mischief years ago, but that too would
be a lie. You don't live in this house now.

The doctors, who know so much, know
less than nothing about your mind. You
aren't a case, prescription, or nurse's order
but a breathing man—father, husband, son—
who planted his garden every spring &
aches to be home from foreign corridors.

Hospital

Room upon room & each
        harbors a character in a book
I won't read. Words pile up
        behind laughter & saline bags.
We gather for her breathing
        thru liquid in her lungs
pain in her left arm, & a sentence
        yet to be framed.

They come & go from
        these beds. I went
to a hillside where I cried
        or a car-ride when we
took our baby home or
        my little writing room
above a yellowwood & road,
        summer rain coming on.

I look too closely at an empty
        bottle on the hospital sill,
berate myself for nothing
        I've ever done but
breathe, reach for one
        more story to tell
at the bedside among
        others wishing her well.

Drum

There comes eventually that moment
after the death watch & the mourning
when you return to your house alone.

The cat's older, house cleared of food
friends & acquaintances brought in offering,
hushed stories of remembered kindnesses

no longer echoing in the narrow space
unused to such crowds. A silence dreaded
& welcome—wider than expected—taut

like a drum or a wire strung along a
highway, like a spent cry heard
again in the mind's upper chamber.

This can't be the end of the poem
nor can anyone read its next lines
scratched lightly on the floorboards.

The Flutist

Wind passing over the lip
water falling 15 feet from
ledge to pool below us.

Goldfinch lights on a purple cone-
flower, searching for seed.
Sunlight heats the present

world hazy, blur where
there ought to be
edge. Wait a minute—I

hear you inching, a thief
flat on roof tile, awaiting your
moment to break & enter.

Work Site

On a journey from the coast to the
interior, I arrived in a small town whose
name I had forgotten. I was supposed to
teach a class there in a park behind a row
of houses. Most of the students I didn't
know, and none seemed interested in
the topic. One young man, however, I
did know. Perhaps he was my son or
someone I remembered from my home
country. He started off enthusiastic

about seeing me again, but soon he gazed off
when I spoke, looking more ashamed than
bored. Occasionally he dozed off. I organized
students in a soccer game, thinking this would
capture their attention, and in fact they began
laughing & cheering at every kick, but the young
man left the class abruptly. I couldn't call to him,
didn't know if he still lingered around the block
or near a corner store. Workers started digging
up the field—backhoe & bulldozer, which
would have pleased my son when he was
a little boy. Now he was gone & I had no
way to reach him. The rest remains a

watercolor wash in blue and rust. Bats
caught their meal overhead as dusk
came on; a hummingbird took one last
sip from red salvia bordering the park.

Nothing settled, nothing quite in place
for the night, but the moon rose anyway
over the abandoned work site.

Wissahickon Creek

The pond's shrinking & scummed over green now
in November where we saw a hundred frogs keep
watch & mate on logs this spring. I follow White
Trail markers along the ridge, scramble down from
beech trunk to maple stump over a stream of dry
leaves that cover stone under roots, to within 50 feet
of the creek. There I go up the dirt & rock Orange Trail,
water on my left, steep forest & schist cliffs on my right.
Crows overhead, I step past sudden patches where rain
has pooled, trickling down toward the Wissahickon. You
would sew this scene onto a cloth dyed madder red:
catalpa frond, rusted carapace among yellow beech
leaves, raccoon scat & mushroom waste embroider the
path I'm on under swirling rock & across the arched
iron cage Fingerspan Bridge to Livezey Lane—its
17th century stone farmstead Glenn Fern, once a grand
mill, now a place to take children on a Sunday—a short
way beyond to Devil's Pool, swimming banned this
year but long a spot for teens to get high & jump
from the rocks. Three geese fly above, rhododendron
still hold their leaves among bare saplings, a mallard
shakes his wet wings under a bowed oak, incessantly
disturbing my unquiet mind. Ahead, a ford over the

stream entering the creek, easy stepping stones today
to the other bank shallow sounds loud against the rock
& pebble bed. The path climbs to a wider view of
the creek thru younger oaks, pale vertical strokes
against slate water, calm here, seeming not to move.

The trail nearing the road admits to more invasion.
Bent trees spray-painted in a white & red code, one
narrow maple tattooed stark blue over lovers' scarred
initials, an abandoned baby carriage propped against a
beech. Black squirrel startles me & skitters up the hill.
I see the County Bridge, geese & ducks gathered like
guests at a wedding in front of Valley Green Inn,
waiting for a toddler to throw them crumbs, her
father warily holding her hand. I cross over the
creek to Forbidden Drive where runners & bikers
rest after their miles. Perhaps I see no more clearly
now, but I can walk back on gravel from here.

From Away

They could tell when I first pronounced
the town name that I was from away.
My clothes didn't fit properly, my accent
designed to single me out. The man who
sold buttons remarked on my gestures, &
soon my hair, my walk, eyebrows, teeth
all became betrayers. Indeed, I found I

didn't belong in my body. The question
preyed on my mind & soon I couldn't eat
without fearing food would go unrecognized
in my belly, or my bowels would refuse to
work under conditions of occupation. My
senses constantly sounded an alarm no
decent brain should answer. Now I wander

around the square into the pretty park
clearly not meant for me. I address the
cold statue standing in her empty pool,
but she merely looks into an upraised
urn as if I had not spoken.

Her House by the River

Time never equals a number
tho you hear seconds pass
like a weight greater than silver.
The tea steeps 3 minutes, back bend
held 30 seconds & a glance
no longer than she takes to pass a plate. Where

does love live in punched walls
shelves crashing, glass shattered, peas
scattered across the tile, fluorescent
glint on vomit in the hot kitchen? Where can

the poem reside? Eyeglasses half folded
on the counter, red sleeveless shirt tossed
down beside the bed, last night's failed
dream conversation I could not recall
while she wandered along another
path to a field of women dancing.

Between our conjured danger
& ugly regress easy to forget
that salient forest where we
sat on a bench, house wren warning & wary
in a box above the rail to our left
& before us a mountain half in
sun, greens dabbed & pooled in sight
below a moving blue hidden a few feet, 200 yards, a mile

narrow as a coffee cup or wide as a month
without end. Not language

after all or even one noun worth pronouncing
in this season of sudden rain
pendulum days to celebrate age
pots thrown on a wheel, glazed now & drying
for the salt-fired kiln. Meantime friends
dance on the grassy yard behind her house by the river.

Boundary Stone

anise purple like a memory

Clarise Lispector

I'm not afraid to speak to you again.
Confabulation & counter-
measures describe an arc I can't
complete yet you remain safe
inside crystal purple shrouding
absence. No proper
conversation with the dead but
words do strain the morning
light. In our rented garden apartment
you stretched out
medics surrounding your head so
I couldn't see & today in cold
summer drizzle I remember the haunts
I've seen you, sensed
you. At that dark lake I talked
to you, only a weathered post next
day. I would weave an open fabric
of visitations, their gaps & fissures, but that
would be a lie, a crumbling wall no
longer holding back the flesh
crusted over then smoothed to scar.
No pride in one-sided
voiced harmonies
when I wept against a rail after rainstorm

perhaps hungover, certainly
ashamed, my marriage already burst
in a tin box. Hardly
your fault you refused to intervene.

You don't impress me
anymore, flicker in the dark or
misremembered picture passport,
letters telling your
mother gentle lies or military orders
sending us to Germany or Georgia.
Still I don't stop calling out to you
powerless as you may be to
interrupt the magic
colloquies that fix a flat or
soothe a burn, roar
in my otherwise empty head
palaver to hammer out
a treaty between live & dead: arid &
expansive, learned & unaware,
flowering & collapsing.

The mind sometimes longs
for a room papered in flocked
florals, potted jade plants on
the sill, tiny figurines arranged
before books any observer could approve
but I can't stay to lobby for a truce. I travel
north & south of an overgrown boundary stone.

Three from Yaddo

Gridded Window

I look out the gridded window—world
thru glass & screen—a dark circle under
that stand of pines & yet there's spotty
snow beneath the dogwood holding
its red leaves despite the freeze. All
words among the things we touch,
all memory covered in light snow, you

walk far from me today, perhaps on
our street. Could we share the same
thought now or is breath always
particulate like coffee grounds in
my empty cup or yellow leaves shed
from a single maple? When I walk
out this door, I see what you can't—
tree trunks smudged in the melting
ice. Where you are, trucks protect
men digging asphalt to get at old
pipes. I can hear their air drills

jackhammering to reach dirt
below even here, where
snowfall makes no sound.

Crust on Snow

In the back acres where
sun won't warm the ground, crazing
frozen puddles after Shane's red
truck left tracks in yesterday's heavy
snow where the lane narrows & turns
sharply back toward cottages. Under
the oaks, downed trees now logs
hollowed out, artillery waiting for shot.
Some would load philosophy, baseball
jokes, physics lessons in those guns. All I

can do is look & yet that too seems rude:
to intrude on wood piles, skip over clods
or ennoble boulders set along the thawing
lake's margin. Nothing but snippets as
one walker stamps his Vibram soles on
slush, noting a previous walker's boot
print. But ahead of me a heavy pine limb
fell, overburdened by last night's storm,
lying in the road impervious to shifts in
the mind of a visitor heading to dinner.

Pond

I found a pond I had neglected these
last days along the lane. A buck's
track crossed the mud & slush to lead
me down a woody hill under a husky
oak that retained its leaves at the top
despite recent winds. His prints
faded into brown fallen leaves thickly
matted, sticks that crumbled rather
than snapped, logs peeling off black
fabric while their inner meat moldered.
Pond ice light green & a fallen pine
like a splinter in a child's eye. I could
build a hut along this inner curve, a
place no one would look for a traveler.

Walks & Dreams

Adesso

for WCW

i.
You've been with me
always (if the clock
starts near 50 yrs
ago) & I wonder

what are you
in lines you left
now in my world
not your own &

yet I see shifting
from stem to edge,
crimson to deadening
desire still obtains

we live in this
obstinate! beside the
point & yet unstable
measure (counting

instants, decades
unreckonable) queered
now by virus & vir-
ulent furies, rapes

economic dis-
possession, banned
gatherings, smiling
grasping captains

of capital & yet
you propose
a variable
shuffle:

absence into dirt
tree dog waterflow
presences—Listen! I
could look past

wars, scorched
blocks, stink neither
flesh nor flower
empty stadia

& you would be
there in the cherry
blossom wet spring
cold purple crocus

tho my season
is autumn the
dying already
accounted for

ii.

"On Oct. 3, 1918, Philadelphia closed all schools, churches, theaters, pool halls and other gathering places. Undertakers were overwhelmed — some funeral homes increased their prices sixfold and some even made the bereaved bury their own dead."

iii.

virus you fought in
your today & yet
you made words
matter anyway

medicine meant ac-
counting to make
a body whole for
a time but scribbling

thinking in lines
sketched, etched
Duchamp glass, a
child breathes

clearer after fever
old woman wobbles
on her feet too
proud to let on

her circumstances
precisely the flesh
of poems, interior
meat of an apple

fallen from an imag-
ined tree beyond a
brick wall enclosing
a neglected garden

iv.
How alone we must all
be, clumps of us ranged
together, organisms

in a Petrie dish or galaxies
stitched on black linen? Distant
or wedded we cling & yet misread

genes or proclivities split us, bells
ring to mark each sect its time to be
isolate or conjoined unmercifully.

Take for example Italy *adesso,* locked
down now, economy collapsing, centuries
of treasure pilgrims savor, wonder

at, pay to see among leather shops & espresso
bars & yet what of the maids & prisoners,

government office workers in their thin

ties? The old ticket taker, staring at her phone
in a booth high inside a duomo tower, barely
notices a few Japanese couples taking selfies.

For Italians dying in hospital corridors, holy
domes turn mausolea, gold mosaic tiles mock
gods & saints, proud artists trumpet a hollow

prophecy that Grace in a meaningless
universe spirals up from the frozen
mouth of Satan to the muscular old Lord.

v.

& yet words form a path I follow
          no matter how mother warned me
                    about the traps sentences can set

neither did Dante learn enough from Virgil
          nor Pound from you. We are lost these
                    days, stumbling around empty lots

poets more drunk than deranged, bound
          to rust like our cars in junk yards
                    echoing incantations for a séance

without visitants, here on this
          warming planet, alone with disease
                    cracked systems, differentials & sunrooms

wild thyme purple in
pavement cracks, twisted pine left
by a bulldozer when it halted for the day

vi.

"The world's eighth biggest economy and its 60 million citizens are under lockdown. Italy became the first European nation to introduce drastic measures controlling the spread of COVID-19. Italy has recorded more deaths from the new coronavirus than China, the origin of the outbreak. In addition to school closures and shuttered shops, businesses are winding down nonessential work and transport hubs are grounding to a halt.

"The Italian government has pledged $28bn to ease the burden of the pandemic. That includes helping companies, homeowners with mortgage payments, and people facing unemployment. Italy really needs all the support it can get right now as it has never really recovered from Europe's debt crisis. Its debt stands close to 135 percent of gross domestic product (GDP) and growth since the introduction of the euro, almost 20 years ago, has barely grown."

vii.

dream curl
starts
barely a wisp
wind over roiling
water

wakes each to
other's inner
satin
tiny snowbells wet
last night's
mist
knee hip
buttocks spine reaching
branches
shoulder blades
breasts, nipples
pebbles in the creek
step rocks
wrist roots splayed
beyond firm hill
soil ex-
postulating crags
blot sky till song, bird
song, spring leaf
song spills
over hair eyes
pooling at shoulders
at bellies, eddying
at thighs we
can't stir
smooth stone
warming in cold
sun

viii.

"Then the flu hit us. We doctors were making up to sixty calls a day. Several of us were knocked out, one of the younger of us died, others caught the thing and we hadn't a thing that was effective in checking that potent poison that was sweeping the world. I lost two young women in their early twenties, the finest physical specimens you could imagine. Those seemed to be hit hardest. They'd be sick one day and gone the next, just like that, fill up and die."

ix.

all we have
    on this chill
        cranky late March
afternoon, forsythia
    dulled by drizzle, dogwood
        a good 2 weeks
away, is magnolia al-
    ready white-pink around
        the corner from our house—
& yet what
    home do we have
        here, tilting now between
bitter branches & flowering
    spring no
        sure consolation as

news pours in
our unbelieving
ears?
Partisans snap
one at another, can't
listen to distress
all around them
for answers, neither
lever nor cudgel
comes easily to
hand. I think, doctor
you would simply
wade into wards
with your fierce
stare & high laugh
neither hero nor
priest, not looking
down nor casting
eyes skyward

willing to breathe
damp air, touch fevered
brows, sing green
ivory lenten rose
hunkered in rain.

Small Hours

You'd think at a time like this
dreaming would come easily—
students spread around a classroom
waiting for a lesson I hadn't prepared

in a field I don't know—but lately my
dreams, intense in the small hours,
merely thin into scrim over morning
coffee by the time I go to write them

down. Only one has survived dawn
in the last week & that more as an
image I have no skill to sketch or
sculpt. I'd sent my family away in

preparation for an attack & then came
a pounding on our thick front door.
I opened in panic & saw, standing
there a figure shimmering in the

dark, no face or limbs distinguishable.
It regarded me with pity, pausing
before it struck. I screamed to drive
the presence off but could make no

sound. Wendy woke me & held me.
I feared to close my eyes again lest
it was waiting, but dreamless sleep
overtook me before it could return.

Cardinal Nest

Walking the neglected corridor where trains
once ran behind these houses & apartments,
we could be in a movie or dream between steep
embankments overgrown with brambles &
tan stalks, our way on the narrow path marked
by motor bike tires in the chocolate dirt. No one
sees us tramping the old rail bed, no disease
from the houses could reach us in the sunny
chill breeze. Insects not yet out, lizards & toads
a month from seeking heat on their skin. We

consider family & friends, remind ourselves of
trails we've walked, sing the words we know
from an old Band song. We shun fear & news
this morning. The track follows a straight line
drawn from one overpass to the next a quarter
mile away, but as we pass brittle thickets
& saplings struggling to stand upright, a female
cardinal sings hard above us, clearly annoyed
we're too close to her nest. The male answers
her & flies sharply by:
Woor-it woor-it
woor-it woor-it.
Cheekita cheekita cheekita.
We don't linger, tho we'd love to see where
she hid in the shrubs not fully green, not fit
shelter for restless ground animals like us.

One Morning

Only this was left from a dream:
I was approaching our town courthouse to
postpone a hearing scheduled for later that
afternoon when I heard a dreadful screech.
I looked up at the courthouse's formal granite
facade & saw, emerging from a hole in the
bottom corner of the pediment, first a rat's
screaming head & then a grey cat shaking
the rat's body from side to side so violently

guts & brains showered the pavement below.
As people gaped on the street, the cat leapt
from the cornice & landed with a thump on
the roof of a dark blue sedan parked beside
me, the rat still screaming but clearly losing
spirit. Scrambling down the hood of the car,
the cat jumped into the air & turned into an
owl, the rat now limp & secure in its claws.
The bird flew with immense wings down

the avenue & away. I walked up the stairs
to the entrance, stepping carefully around
bits of rat before the double glass doors
that led to court offices.

Side Streets

Snow on side streets narrows
heart's arteries to alleys.
Quarantined in two rooms

the knitter barely able to fit
her walker thru a channel
walled by magazines & news

moves from sitting room to
bed, kidney bean cans &
Ritz cracker packs

stacked on kitchen counter. *Set*
the box anywhere, she says,
do I know you? Roads

lead to store but she's
not taking that trip anymore—
payment late, landlord

might lock her out, drop
her things on pavement
tree roots jacked up.

Outside I watch robins
feast on berries they find
in vines wrapping dead

oaks along old railroad
tracks. Shoe shop shuttered
but next door they still

sell coffee & damp doughnuts.
I listen to sparrows fuss & a
woodpecker searches for grubs.

Sequestered

I dreamt we were sequestered in a cabin surrounded
by forest. In addition to the general crisis, some
personal or local tragedy hung over us despite
the sun & spring blooms outside our front
porch. A woman about our age came to us &
announced she was moving in. She could have
been an acquaintance from long ago, but neither
of us remembered her. She showed no interest in
us & yet seemed exhilarated to be in our house
& woods. The next morning, she began to walk

about our rooms & then out into the yard shadowed
by trees, hanging fabric & arranging our belongings
so that everything seemed astonishingly new. One
cloth caught the light in such a way I'd never seen
before, flapping & folding so that red & ochre
contrasted with violent shapes changing each
moment. The visitor seemed entranced by what
she saw, & she kept up her activities all day till
the three of us were exhausted. Her appreciation
infected us; we had no energy to suspect her

gleeful attention to the tiniest object. The next
day she moved about our space with equal
delight, every minute discovering another marvel
in ordinary things. The third day she awoke late,
hardly able to lift her head; we felt obliged to
take over her duties, showing her corners of
her room she hadn't explored & figurines

that might bring her delight. By the fourth day, she had disappeared or perhaps the dream ended before either of us noticed she'd gone.

Saylor's Grove

Leaving the shadows in the park, we walked
along Lincoln Drive, cars ripping past us after
our rambling pace among half dozen walkers
on the wide path beside the creek. We waited
for the light 10 feet from a couple who, like
us, wore masks. When the light changed, we

all crossed Lincoln to a wooded triangular
tract defined by three streets that hid a
wetland few ever stop to see. The couple
continued up Rittenhouse Hill, but we entered
the narrow marsh where a dark pond held
hundreds of orange carp. Beer cans & chip

bags in mud at the margins, we stepped past
dry grass & discovered a stand of cattail reeds
& an island, no bigger than a stranded van.
A struggling cleft tree grew there, magnificent
only in its reflection overlaying koi in knotted
throngs beneath the stubbled surface of the green

pool. The City had laid flagstone nearby, now
overgrown, on which a goose nestled heedless
of our voices. Round the other side, they'd built
a walled deck to view the brook that fed
the carp pond. A place to stop, a place to

stop the world! From there we could watch
red-winged blackbirds, cone-beaked fliers
shrugging their patched shoulders, screech
on scruffy branches & cattail spires.

One Afternoon

Young detective reads us his commendation from the boss
Shoppers masked in line along the produce market parking lot
White plastic laundry basket half full
Walk & walk but what's she pointing at among the pines
Stone library unlit, no chairs in sight
Widowed mother tells me wait, my VW Bug running outside
Petal drying on brick below pink azalea
Tug towing a barge of split-leaf maple
Amber buildings & blue-grey streets without a soul

Arms paralyzed across my chest

Bronze & Emerald

Bronze & emerald in filtered
sun, immobile on a
knotted branch anchored in
just enough water for
bugs to skate & oaks to
reflect around him, his globe
slows to a century's
unblinking black gem
set between rippled rock

& tattered log, light
shattered by a child's
boot & then his sister's
plash, tadpoles they
seek they seldom
catch in nets. Mother
watches from the bank
not wanting to intrude
but, like the frog, waits

for her moment. We
re-visit this pond often
to see emerging habitants,
old trunks shed bark
new duckweed bloom
after freezing & drying
winter. We register
first croaks, jays manic
in their ministry, a purple

grackle hopping from stick
        to pole to rock & above
                hawk draws us larger
circles. None can
        enter another's inner
                stirrings: young maples, great
cracked beech, tulip
        poplars towering but
                one day wind will rip

this or that tall character
        down whole by the roots
                creek wear ribbed rocks
smooth beneath the high
        arched Henry Avenue
                Bridge, its traffic muted
here where we sit
        beside frog & grackle's
                muddy little pond.

Yahrzeits

Giselle

Giselle her real name, she took out
trash in their building & picked
up icons—jelly jar, dented pewter
cup, bent spoon—she could set

beside her needlework. My cousins
warned me she would lie to get her
way but I sent her poems. Surely
she'd recognize me standing outside

her father's inn as they fled pistols
& flame long before the Nazis came
to Hungary? Her brother joined the
Resistance & became a Communist;

she mourned him alongside the dead
in camps. Bubbe served paprikash &
kugel, ate chicken feet for breakfast
& told me milk cured her mother

of TB. My mother was a shiksa
to her, never capable of keeping
a kosher home, the thief who stole
her son away & then let him die.

Cleveland papers screamed her name
when Bubbe refused to rent to a white
woman with a black husband. She moved
to Jerusalem, had a heart attack cooking

for Shabbos & set fire to her kitchen.
Neighbors revived her but she refused
medical care for fear doctors
would kill her with their drugs.

Tremont Temple
for SK

I remember Max as an old wrestler—not like my
father's father, slender with beard & payos—but
stubbly jaw & short stature, stocky & bald. New

York was Max & Lillian's 3-room apartment just off
the elevator in a Morningside Heights high rise. Heavy
end tables & brocade sofas accommodated aunts &

uncles at our farewell party before the Army sent us
to Germany when the Wall went up. Family histories
I didn't know: Mary & Herman who could cha-cha,

teacher Belle, who mailed us books, married to
marine engineer Dave, a Greek Jew, & glamorous
Toby married to cigar scented Ben. Eldest Pauline

scared me with her regal cane. I met them all &
knew none. But Grandpa Max, who told jokes &
built shelves that would never fall, Brotherhood

president at Tremont Temple (before they
abandoned the Bronx), drove a Fleetwood black
Cadillac & thought art a waste of time except

my mother's piano playing. She stopped
concertizing at 16 when she went to college
& never lived home again.

Reading about Einstein
for LL

At 11 I found a book
in the library about Einstein.
No other story meant
so much, tho opposites
Christy Mathewson &
Dizzy Dean both threw
shutouts & Tecumseh
led battles against
white settlers, Florence
Nightingale cared
for wounded soldiers
my father might have
stitched up, but here
was a Jew bullied & dis-
missed in school, gaining
fame by explaining how
stars curve straight
lines or what a boy
on a hill could see at
either end of a train
approaching the speed of light.

Like young Einstein,
I wanted to imagine
orbits & white heat
neglect my worksheets
forget my socks.
Secret forces in massive

bodies or specks whirling
        around tiny suns meant
Boy Scouts or Little
        League or marbles on vacant
lots didn't measure
        up to gravity or time.
Then Nazis' hate & the
        bomb's chain reaction.
I feared him
        & desired his life.

Jew therefore unlike, small
        therefore unchosen, chubby
therefore unlovely. Thinking
        might do the trick, might
carry me past Army
        barbed wire, over
the heads of beer drinkers
        choking on hard Ks &
gargling their vowels
        to a world where
balls drop up
        & apes do not age.

White Jeans

I saw his legs in white jeans, then red
lower half of a turtleneck, but medics
gathered round his head & shoulders
administering oxygen & pounding on
his chest. They herded us into a station
wagon & drove us to the Krells' house—
light brick & dark wood trim, neat
suburban street—far from that shitty
ground floor apartment we'd landed
in only a month before. Nothing to say

this year, in English or Hebrew, but I lit
the candle in hopes it would shed light
on today's trauma & loss, sparrows frantic
at the bird feeder, troops massing against

protest: the weather changes
but he's been gone too long.

Whatever I feel passes thru him, skein
too tangled for weaving, shucked
husk ready for compost, translucent
skin sheltering us neither from fire
nor rain. Workmen clatter, assemble
concrete forms for a new foundation
down the block, a house some family
will spoil or grace, spray champagne
& grill their chicken on the deck.

You'd think after 55 years I'd have
something to say, but no. Let the
candle burn till it gutters out.

At Carpenter's Woods

As we stepped down the path from root
        to rock edge, a bare trickle in the creek
flowed to meet the stream that joins
        the Wissahickon further on. We sat
on a bench beneath a scarred beech,
        not noticing at first the plaque for
Blaine, our son's friend gunned down
        years ago on a corner because he looked
like another dark-skinned teen a gang
        wanted dead. We watched the stream,
children playing on a bridge nearby,
        shade & haze hiding early heat, catbird
& red-eyed vireo singing hieroglyphics.

Andorra Meadow

Mid-morning late October, we wish a happy
Halloween to masked walkers & their costumed
dogs who pass us on the trail. Sun shines
but doesn't warm the air. Election threats,

police murder, lost jobs like foul smoke
after fire over the park but here sparrows
still shift from cherry sapling to pioneer
beech above grasses that stand or lie flat,

marking storms & bad dreams that rolled
thru last week. An abandoned bluebird box
alone in the meadow recalls summer's heat
& plenty. Now black walnuts gnawed open

litter the ground, soon to be bleached by
freezing rain. As we near the road we hear
hammers at work on new condos. We
turn away, seeking cold shade under

tattered catalpas at the meadow's edge.
You & I remember what we try
to forget at the margins. Dry yellow
maple leaves against damp soil imprint

afterimages when I blink but I must
watch my step over roots & jutting stone
on the path down to the drive where
runners gather for afternoon practice.

Weathered Bench

At the end of Woodbrook, post & pole
fencing opens to a loop trail under
beech & maple that leads to a spot
above a creek littered with beer cans.
Fallen trees caught in the forks of leafless
storm survivors cross over my head &
bent branches complicate the white
sky. I stand beside a weathered bench
overlooking the weak brook—it's too
cold to sit this afternoon—wondering

how long Wendy's mother can live
alone denying her need for help or
comfort. Neighbors walk their dogs here
mornings & evenings but I'm by myself
today. Even the spotted lantern flies
we saw in summer, massed congregants
on the body of two sweetgums along
the path, are gone now. They left
only black sooty mold at the roots
& eggs that will hatch in the spring.

Late July

They say storm's coming in, perhaps
tornado. Our garden needs rain.
Still trees with their sooty knees
hunch above the pocked street, pods
& branchlets torn off & scattered by
quickening wind across pebbled

sidewalk beside a blue Honda where
one woman hides & hoards herself.
Replanted hill slants down from old
manse painted sickly yellow. Here a
sign proclaims their child graduated,
there I know a grandmother died

choking last month in a sealed
ward. Dirty red pickup won't stop
but black Mercedes glides to a halt.
My left leg aches on this long walk.
I nod to a mother in Kente cloth
pushing her tiny son in a carriage

shaped like a brown egg, everyone
hurrying home before the clouds break.
I can hardly breathe for sad rage;
sparrows shift from sweetgum to oak
to pine. A crow cries out in a sparse
dying sycamore as the hot sun sets.

Can't forget

Can't forget
the stairwell
filling with
rain & I
had to get
to the store-
room below—

insistent
desire for
opening.

Unjust Sonnets

Illusions Clothe

To cut thru things around us—this gentle
surgery always at hand, incited by scent or red
scarf or blue rough hand towel—not memory
alone nor lingering regret but a fresh trail in
faint snow, katsura leaf caught on a drying
weed stem, full moon yellowed on late
December horizon line. Fire sirens from
3 blocks away mark bright henna scars
across my cheek. Bribes & duplicity, anger

& hate: illusions clothe passengers on the
bus, cops patrolling the pitted avenue, even
a little trembling dog held in his ancient
owner's arms as they enter the Rite Aid
at Walnut Lane. Blankets & screens,
scaffolding & brackets, wheeled walkers
& carved canes. I look up at lights around
Vision Works, down at the slab lifted by
a curbside maple. I'm afraid of falling &

I fall into the cauldron dyeing heavy cotton
weave an iron orange, repeated figures
dance at the hem neither precious nor
coarse. I choose the middle path to govern
spirits when I cry out in dream, banishing
abandoned children from our rooms.

Candle Music

No desire for
enlightenment
                              when I'm dead never
to touch faces I love
               nor witness disgrace
               I think I should
resist or applaud. Daylight
becomes night becomes day—
sameness shatters
                              screeching or secret
glass shards, drama
               sudden & exit fast—cicada
               drone beneath empty sky.
Too grateful to
                              accept I'll lose them all.

Others can lead the march or
mark rage occasions, hard
as I may try to heap dirt on
                              barricades or lob clods
at enemy heads. Nor will I
               perfect my psyche, expect
               a cure for dream ailments
or cancel imagined debts.

Red traces led me
                              into & out of houses
where I sheltered,
to long walks years

ago in dry grass on
California rounded hills
French prune orchard
in the valley below
portraits framed
by a matchstick barn
long before fires took them all.

Sing a bright song
dance the path
sheep crop in
ripening meadows,
etched copper
cuffs on the slender
arm of a wrathful
sprite, a chant you
recite but can't
recall: candle music
burned them all.

Faces

We poured our wine & gathered
round the outdoor table, filled
plates & talked into the afternoon.
Cherry in bloom above us, garden
plot fenced behind not yet dug,
the sun grew hot as we told
our stories, joked about isolation,
caught up on kids, revealed
work changes & shared griefs.
We'd watched each other's faces
grow lined & longer but no less

light for all the strain, time
marked not in years but brush
strokes of deeper reds & purple,
gestures enacting deft motion,
kindness now a fold above
the eyebrow. Early evening
grew cooler & we retired
inside, sharing almond
cookies & tea, talk become
a secluded pond, leave
taking delicious & sad.

For Jim & Peter

We three talked away an afternoon
watching blossoms fall on the merry

spring throng in Washington Square
so soon after the long, diseased winter.

Stumble around Ruins

Broken brick beside a stony road
mauve shadows settle rough block
signals molded to melody stitched
under the chin, memory bringing

back blows: sudden rancor in an
alcove reserved for rest. Maunder
over empty pockets, grave newly
scratched can't heal the dead.

No light but dim stars in unmown
fields, tumbled rock sheltering cats.
Pilgrims seeking release from history
only have to state the obvious.

Ringing a bell struck years ago, they
congregate, eyes lowered to the marble
entrance barred & locked, pour red
wine into mud holes rain turns

into lavender ponds encroaching on
high grass. Scrabble about for that lost
tooth, transmute mutter to song, & shame
soaks like butter into hot dark bread.

A young beech breaks your descent
on the steep path punctured by frozen
rivulets leaked from the street sewer.
Don't deny yourself a muffin & water

when you rest on a log. Hammer your way out of the pit, away from traffic & construction. Only a drunk calling out before dawn saves your little heaven.

After Soutine

Words we spoke melt
        into the creek while eyes
                pursue trails thru
hillside saplings,
        drama repeated at
                dawn when a match
can't light fire
        nor tea suffuse
                cold water.

Strokes in red & teal
        carve splotched
                canvas, grotesques gaze
behind flawed glass into
        our home, funereal
                rites won't halt phrases
dissolving on the stream,
        dream's abrupt sunlight
                corrupting absent faces.

Messengers

You would not know our
worlds, we are so
in yours. Entrance
& farewell, citadel &
tilled field, blatant sun
or shaded trail: neither

mask nor stolen words
stand for creatures
hidden in garden alcove
nor lend cover for those
who walk in pairs or
shamble alone, foreground

now backdrop, flute
motif forming the recess
called your eye.
Turtle settles beside
smaller others on canal
log, heron searches

muddy bottom, May
sun heats afternoon
reeds & the brick
heaped there. Keep
all passages open
a moment longer, won't

you, mother? Surely
you depart before sleep.

Pose for Photos

Don’t resist that dusty hideout
beside a stream behind houses
you hate. Very little counts: only
words between death & a splendid
getaway. What a war machine!

A breast pocket contains pills for
plague & gout. You’re not an expert
in cloudy weather; speaking may
be out of the question. Yet the lecture
hall awaits & guests arrive from

an ancient city some generations
south of here. Shopkeepers—
earning sums daily but still falling
into debt—pose for photos at the
bank, cruel sunlight on their bare

legs, torsos turn from off-key
music (trumpet players getting
away with murder at the dance-
hall). A gentle basso overhead
etches blue plane into pink cloud.

I Met a Man

I met a man who said
in a crushed voice he
found nothing to lift
his eyes from the carpet

these days. We ate cheese
& crackers. Across the street
oaks dropped acorns on
stumps left by last year's

culling, children leapt
into soaked tree mulch,
parents pushed carriages
outside homes built before

their grandfathers were born.
He must have seen the joke
to say: "What do you do
for fun?" & I wriggled like

a worm washed onto hot
sidewalk after rain, replying
I had no time till spring when
we planned to travel. Wine

Soured, wind whisked bats
high into white dusk then,
before anybody spoke, they
swooped low at our heads.

Eye Carved

Eye carved in soft stone
half horse profile half
clinging vine repeated
up old temple edge—no
longer locale for awe
or prayer, refuge or
judgement—now only
winged little minds
nest in shading maple.

Evening brings no
disaster, small shower falls
sweet after downpour.
I trust the weather
but resist the mood:
groan in loose gutter,
cranky dog left
outside, plane trees shake
droplets onto a fitful street.

I can't calibrate
the metronome or
ignore the barely
concealed samba beat
containing an ordinary god.
Cashier ringing up the bill
comforts me: numbers
confirm the vision
delivered a day too late.

Everything Along

Everything along the way:
red digital time by
the bed, bridge across
the creek, small birds' seeping
oratory among trees that hold
up a few leaves against
autumn sun. Single effort
counts for little—bans
on gatherings empty
once packed squares,
soldiers hunch in camouflaged
tanks, the hatches shut
but ready—a stray soul
willing to exist stings
the eye; blackout affords
no claim to victimhood
& none show up for
inquests, court shuttered
shops boarded up against
wind lifting discarded
placards & stained
pizza boxes, pink threads.
Many blame one beast
or another but who
saw what
happened when
the curtain tore.

Sluice

Down broken stone patch
sluice autumn creek bloody
maple leaves, dry wishes
pulverized underfoot

Beech fallen across a span
murmur weeks & first
cold, sewn & cut, gap
like a mallet beating time

Slow growing slime & shelf
mushrooms mark the log's
long arm braced for wreck
leukemic cells argue dark

Future face steamed
on bath mirror, shell
hidden in water flowing
one way limpid & bitter

Moist Clay

Fingers shape moist
clay into fired form

wine meant to soften
hard edge of waiting

releases nothing, nor do
birds sing this afternoon

when a son answers
his own questions

Signs

i

among brown beech
leaves hanging in fog
mosaic trunks, wilted
bracken, four empty

chairs left to weather
rain another season,
carpet pattern suffered
below half-light on

uneven ground, gust
music measured in
sparrow flight, grey
enveloping fools cast

quickly, quick omen
grain milled on stone
for bread medicinal,
hand more claw than tool

ii

same beech leaves
in darkening rain grow
yellow against hemlock
scrim faded to mist

friends cooking stew
quiet wine laughter
reaches me here down
stairs by the fire while

I recall photos taken
in another city, river
we crossed to see cold
shadow stern towers

traveling then, no
fear we have today
our disease leaves
distance itself a sign

iii

early December sun
sere winter melody
dark slash on bright
slanted light pooled

at the roots of beech,
hemlock, unsheathed
oak & maple, a dead
birch under sketched

clouds moving across
weak blue heaven
hemlocks infested, dying
like the ash, wind &

sun shifting around us
we walk the trails as
if we can do no more
than consume nothing

iv

light alters foot by
foot this afternoon
behind hemlocks
dry beech leaves

shivering in barren
brown breeze earth
moves as clouds do
washed down stream

sun drifts off stage
no day like this
day we set blue
trail blaze on trees

we may not live to
see die or die
before us sketched
on white evening

Arch

I put brush to paper
feel the tense surface
then scrawl dissolves
fine finish, leaving
on empty expanse only
wordless marks framing
ground peopled by shadows:
mice move there, ants
& beetles, but from this
distance nothing seems
to inhabit grass & gravel
beside a stone arch,
reminder of forgotten
victory over a people.
See, their candelabrum
hoisted above soldiers'
heads! Armored bodies
crowd the frieze, only
cloth from desecrated
temples trampled beneath
the mob's feet signify
those crushed by disease
& superior arms. I didn't
mean to honor conquest.

Started to cook dinner

& then died: couldn't
        stir the sauce, wash
                a plate, touch your
cheek except as an
        unfelt breeze. Upstairs
                books remained unopen
pen capped & incapable
        of leaving a mark & so,
                diminished, I was gone.

Now at War

Army town keeps bodies
on ice behind garages where
GI's fix trucks & hours slip by
while mechanics smoke.

Officers issue sticks to clash
about the yard. No danger
from live weapons or targeted
shelling—you just feel the swell

before the wave—the wave
itself may come & go un-
heeded. We're too busy
holding our heads above

water: thousands dead,
5 million fled the country.

Sparrows

Cresting the bridge, a van bears
down on me. Sparrows, jays, robins
sing in budding trees, gardener
stops her digging, roofer holds
his hammer above his shoulder,
child drops her yellow doll. Cross
walk means little, sun means
less than steel on bone or glass
shattering the driver's skull.
                                        Should I
take back what I said to you this
morning or ponder again sage
green wall in my breathing:
nothing happens in that field I see
of phlox & mustard flower, Queen
Anne's lace at the border ditch
where a dead muskrat lies shaded
by blackberry shoots, sky
cloudless blue, railroad tracks
mute below rebuilt bridge. I
mind the ticks in high weeds.

The Colorist

after Milton Avery

Hand shapes a landscape
jealous sand by burning blue
painter paints a poet painting:
birdsong welter, street clamor
iron graves dug in a womb
blistered staves mark melody

in time. Savory green behind
a purple table, outside the open
window grey gaggle of angry
novitiates possess briny
fedoras, sport ruby rings
squeeze fictive lavender

blood seething among lilies &
violets. Once distilled, yellow
goes down like silt beside
azure brushed over angry red.
Never entirely flat, drunk
autumn pastures carry on

their backs some trees, scrawled
like Hebrew script offered to a
distanced God & hosts. Daughter,
however, holds black cat chaos
on her teal lap while she gazes
eyeless, parchment & crimson

back at Father.

Unjust Sonnets

No Matter

Below black walnut trees, I slipped on hidden
sticks among weeds & fell backward in slow
motion, the red brown path above my head,
a patch of aconite wet against blue t-shirt
& grey hair. Dangerous fall for an old man
but for me hardly a scratch, no matter for
concern. I jumped up laughing, brushed
off my hands & shook rain from my pants,
but in my mind I kept falling as we walked
downhill & back to the car—hospital bed,
x-rays, spinal surgery, pain meds. Still,
no need for remedies beyond tea &
leftover salmon on toast. Reader, refrain
from worry over falls in unjust worlds.

Two Mice

I came downstairs this morning to
find two baby mice dead on the dining
room floor. Turds, I thought at first, tho
I remembered soon enough we'd buried
our last cat years ago. One beside the
other, the mice looked arrayed like
tiny cadavers destined for anatomy
lab. I swept each body into a dented
dustpan, carried them out to a corner
of the yard where in summer we pile
pulled weeds &, in the fall, dry leaves.
Don't expect insight among discarded
green matter: just two mice dead
without ceremony or solid reason.

Weak Knees

Weak knees won't carry the weight
these days—must be strong to keep
from screaming—yesterday a casket,
tomorrow muck nearly to the roof.
Strong winds rip branches from old
street sycamores the city needs to cut
down & bullets pierce spring jackets
at the market a block away. Backhoes
& jack hammers tear up concrete
beside the railroad bridge rusting
since the line no longer runs. Shut
your eyes, little sister, till slow cars
pass our corner & we can pretend
all we wanted was gum at the store.

Rock Rift

Rock rift above molten slush, gravel
crushed between iron plates, all I can
utter belongs within this thimble, wishes
swell to cries, rhythm wells up from
timber gorge, memory erased & crashed
among bricks & cinders. Abandoned
diner—its punched-out windows & red
graffiti flicked over plywood sheathing,
notes on a spreadsheet—recalls last plague,
bruises left on flesh for next banquet
floating ammonia wrapping the planet.
Fire ants crowd fat peonies, bow to gone
priests & rabbis, peel back scarlet petals
for nectar secreted out of mutual desire.

Damn Minute

Just wait a damn minute, I'm thinking
the same dream: stroll along forest's
ancient pike, quarry on right, swollen
stream left, toads & fern, jewelweed
& climbing ivy under oaks. Back on
hard luck news flash—floating crapshoot
brickbats tossed by garish candidates—
passengers witness a young starling
fall from her nest, kicks then stops as
the train pulls in. Up bright summer
avenue red-purple striped underwear
mummers blare their horns, bang bass
& snare, while willows overhead drink
vertigo from seepage in sealed tunnels.

Red Lettuce

Wrinkles at our eyes, forehead plowed rows,
creases bracket lips: we mirror each other as
we kiss, laughing past shadow in stories.
Hands meet in wicked sidewalk heat, seek
shade under tulip poplars dropping greenish
yellow flower cups beside raised beds where
neighbors grow kale, red lettuce, pole beans,
tomatoes, cabbage, collards, squash. Young
parents try holding toddlers back, nurses
wheel old travelers along paths between
blue phlox & raspberry, chickens inspect
their common plot. Storm soon, fierce
wind may bring that dead oak down but
no one flees the heavy sun for dark rooms.

Dove Calls

Crown crow spies, hummingbird tongue
tells the tally of crime & grief: thick
trunk cedars gone for brief-lived lawns,
needles in Kensington alley spattered
with spew, rounds fired into South St.
throng. House wren scolds song over
news bleed; neither axle nor pistol,
writ nor custom, strike nor slow down,
bottle cap nor barricade can stanch the
flow. Some might say nobody's wrong
if everybody shuts up, hates the job but
can't quit. How else pay for velvet drapes,
baby formula, swollen feet? Retreat to
real dream when mourning dove calls.

Knotweed

Stepping the narrow trail over wet rock slabs
& slick roots, I avoid falling but douse my boots
in sudden stream & then climb past boulders
before a cave some hermit could use for refuge
during war. Tulip poplar straight above basswood,
alders along the mucky creek—texts forming
history—block roar & truck dust on the drive
below. Emerging from shade, I cross traffic &
slip thru broken chain link fence gate, up gravel
incline to the corridor left when train crews
tore out rails. Shoulder high knotweed flowers
in rising planet fever; ailanthus, poison ivy,
burdock, nettle, vetch among fruitless grape
so dense dirt bikes can't rip tracks in this heat.

Shut Door

I look into mirror no mirror, hostile
house where no one uses language
or credits gesture, simile, snort with
sense. Tone commands panic, sibilant
consent. Distrust follows me as I enter,
nudges me on stage, assigns me a role
in drama where one speaker shouts
against another then binds himself to
his own chair. I cover my ears, wait for
music to end Act 1, usher leads me out,
shuts the great exit door on all protest.
Threats mean nothing. No costume, no
song, no dinner lovingly prepared can
penetrate the utter silence in that mirror.

Pine Grove

For a time maple, oak, poplar give way
To pine above the upper trail. Dry needles,
ten thousand pencil marks in white dark
soil—far from gunfire & shrill disease,
away from family dreams that trouble
sleep—muffle my steps as birds sing
the grove alive: breathe & walk, breathe
& walk. Later beech, sweetgum, birch
line the wider way down toward the ford,
a biker speeds by me over brick debris &
broken concrete, traces of the road to farms
along the hill where soldiers fought once
&, knowing the scuffles & screams today, I
swear I'll hear shots on our street tonight.

Just So

Just so, the reader concludes & sibs
join hands over an ash-filled pot. Porch
swing cries louder than sparrow notes
chipping air sharp & a week's groceries
sit forgotten on the front step. Kids
scatter to play ball or freeze tag, day
trundles toward summer twilight till
somebody's hit by a pitch she didn't
see coming & everybody goes home.
Simple dinner quickly gone except
one dawdler holds up the crew & then
they're running again into the dark,
each to a tune no one else can hear,
sixty years alone among each other.

Town Courts

Fire no fire in these woods where rage
can't enter when rain falls heavy on beech
leaves, drips onto holly, hornbeam, black
locust to sassafras, viburnum to trillium
sedge, fern & plantain at the trail's edge.
Forest burned before, flame spread up
vines & shrubs, driving off crow, snake,
chipmunk, spider but now town courts
scorch brick walls, high windows draped
in edicts no one can unbind. Broad barked
trunks deaden public lies, we grow quiet
walking under maple shade to water
shaping mica schist & quartzite, neither
question nor answer in that fierce music.

Love Fall

Love, neither color nor number—neither
way station nor destination but rhythm
in walking or scene in dream—can hold
fear off as raspberry thorns whip my palms
& I fall from the path into half-dried wrist
thick branches cracked from downed pine,
vicious ivy & Virginia creeper over birch
stumps, & tumble to rest in a pit-mound
left by uprooted sycamore bridging the
stream. Love. Did love trip you or save
you, broken headed traveler, alive in a
ditch the wind dug when storm deranged
this hillside? Above blue jay's strict bray,
wood thrush quick notes clear the mind.

Scant Rooms

Little sister, you witnessed it all: father
dead, mother cocooned & spinning threads
from her very body. Brother & I walked
away, following our paths, but you stayed
for weaving, laving, wrapping, interring.
We lit no candles; you kept a shrine & still
keep it, inventing what we forgot. Late
August brought no rain to the dusty field
outside the scant rooms Mom rented for his
final day, his show re-running on black &
white screens every night at five when ten
thousand coffins shipped home couldn't
replace his body bag. Curled dry bark at
the trail head, grief crunching underfoot.

Coda

Below black walnut trees, I slipped on two
tiny cadavers destined for anatomy lab. Weak
knees won't carry the weight these days: all I
can utter belongs within this thimble, willows
overhead drink vertigo from seepage in sealed
tunnels. Hands meet in wicked sidewalk heat,
house wren scolds song over news bleed, knot-
weed flowers in rising planet fever. I look into
mirror no mirror, hostile house muffles steps
as birds sing the grove alive till somebody's
hit by a pitch. Fire no fire in these woods
rage can't enter. Did love trip you or save
you, broken traveler? Little sister heard
curled dry grief crunching underfoot.

Circle

Hybrid Contusions

House sounds rise & fall at night, dead
leaf scratches on the windowpane, mouse
drags a vegetable peel toward his hole
behind the stove, radiators retreat from
earlier heat. In the dark I overhear my duty:
infant asleep at 2 weeks sets fire to city limits,
bread at the coop turns to straw again, a
friend forswears cancer but no one stops

missile strikes & police beat a man to death.
Reports trickle into our pine grove quarters—
wind carries marching orders mumbled from
jaws taped shut—I'm unable to move my chair
even an inch from the edge. Storm brings wet
horizon closer to sibylline undergrowth & crow
beaks clatter from tree limbs two months away
from budding, away from hybrid contusions.

Woodcut

No print is complete in itself, it
is one more stake in the ground.
Shiko Munakata

You wear a blood red fleece jacket
as you sketch bare trees marking
the celadon sky. I would only
jumble words, make farce of this
scene but you, gouging curled
wood from a tempered board,
call up a draped figure thrown
beside the torrent, rocks channel
water but can't hold back
that flow, wind tips old beech
leaves but oak limbs don't move,
cliff overlooks a narrow path eyes
can't see, melody repeats on a
wooden flute, steps die away
& voices fade. You follow
unnoticed, hoping to prevent
what now will surely happen.

Wind

Wind coming in from the west
brings sparse snow to weedy
yards & uncleared brambles.
Firemen in long roaring trucks

roll down one street bound
for rescue, sirens stopping cars
kids kicking a ball or digging for
treasure in vacant lots, mothers

pushing infants tucked into
carriages that bounce over
pitted walks & swerve
around black plastic bins

upended after morning
pickup. I picture streets
blocked by concrete slabs &
glass shards in cities at war:

children dropping rubble down
holes, mothers walking babies in
smoky frigid air after yet another
attack from distant outposts.

For all our furor
we destroy each other
leaving only mounds of
spoiled abandoned dirt.

Mid-week I went

to a party where no one spoke to me or
knew my name. A great vase holding
Peruvian lilies swelled to the dining room
ceiling, curtains blocked the last evening
light. I had planned to leave before sunset
but could locate no door or even a hallway
leading to another part of the increasingly
complicated house. Guests grew quiet then
disappeared altogether, music welled up.
I seemed to be alone but soon I heard
voices, toasts, laughing by a pond perhaps
outside if I could only find a window that
overlooked the garden. These are not my
people, I thought, I can't eat their food
or drink their wine, but I was so hungry
& needed rest, if only for a moment,
before starting on my journey to a town
where I promised to teach a lesson
I haven't yet begun to learn myself.

Commotion

Fears enter the room. Dark
windows don't bother me, nor
trees scraping branches & new
leaves against roof tiles. I let

commotion go with my breath
won't heed ghosts or news that
sit with me while I prepare for
sleep. They say that presence

looms above others too from earlier
troubles: eyes more silver, brow
shaded by unbrushed curls. Who
knows what I gained from him,

what I lost at his hand? The storm
quiets; hurt children cry in the wind.
No dreams but perhaps I can doze
hours still before morning bird song.

Sudden freeze

Sudden freeze along the creek, mud
dashed rock, ice patches, desire
pulls us up short, stroke mentioned
in casual conversation. A crow calls
from ailing sycamore, row home

roof slumps to the right.
These days it's all waiting—
tea cups fill & then empty, bread
once fresh needs toasting—I could
not carry on without you.

I take two steps toward crossing
without assurance that stones
will hold my weight. Creek looks
cold, trail steeper on the other side.
Poplars reach branches, no leaves.

Circle

Not to get out of the circle
but to come into it in the right way.
Martin Heidegger

Adjacent

Anger built from spoken word
heard in a cauldron, untended
desire confounds circuits
& shuts down house power.
Enter the room—fire light your
only guide, eyes require time

to adjust—hollow stemmed
glass tulips in a salt-fired vase
on a round dining table
set for four old friends.
Outside a truck backs
up, chainsaw cuts down

our long-dead tree. Jet
overhead goes east
toward adjacent ocean.
Across the street children
scream & play ball behind
high fences while in

another country kids
also scream. No one
attending this meal can

stand outside our circle
pursuing years without
end. We begin again.

Tangent

Walking today my usual route
over autumn spatter—yellow
stars, dun oak palms upturned
red split maple leaf mat & pale
gingko fans, their stinking berries—
I tune to news on my ear buds:

limited prisoner exchange amid
bombing pause, UN reports
little world effort to stop planet
warming, 6 shot on a drug corner
blocks from my old school. I step
past wet neat whale humps blown

& raked to the curb, waiting for
city machines to sweep them off
our streets. At Locals Cafe, the
Air Force vet who drove an Uber
lectures me again about war &
money till I pack up & leave. Of

course, news dates my poem
consigns words to the compost bin.
Mere broth fit for a baby. Spun
yarn unraveled when an ancient
knitter nods off, her scarf just
garbled color in uneven rows.

Chord

All very well to have needs but what will
rowing out on the lake get you as the wind
picks up & clouds grow fierce? A moment
ago you were on the shore debating whether
or not to shove off, figuring you had a good
hour of daylight left, but now you're pulling

at the oars against heavy weather, trying
to cross over to that little cottage above
a distant dock even tho you don't know
if they even want a visit. Probably they
already lit the fire & set out the soup
without you since you never told them

you were coming by. You only met the old
couple yesterday at the opening in town
when nobody seemed to have anything to
say to each other & you told that pointless
story about your mother's last year. Will
you even be able to find the dock in the

dark & wet & cold by the time you row
across the lake? What will you say when
they open the door? You can offer that bottle
you stashed in your backpack but they'll
know right away the wine was cheap. Will
anybody care after the attack at the college,

two young girls dead & fourteen in intensive
care? Maybe they'll drink whatever swill
you bring just to be nice. Nobody wants
to be alone on a night like this, or any night
after a shooting right in front of you,
the revolver so close to your head.

On Our Drive

On our drive to return our 14-month-old grandson, Andre, to his parents' home in a part of Philadelphia some 40 minutes from our house, we pass Northeast High School at Algon and Cottman Avenues. If they stay where they are, Andre might someday go to this large brick complex, a relatively smooth functioning school in the chronically underfunded District. Less than a mile from Northeast, we pass the intersection called Five Corners, where SEPTA buses stop to pick up kids going home at 3 PM.

One afternoon in March, as throngs of kids climbed into buses at Five Corners for the ride home, three young men in masks jumped out of a blue Hyundai and fired more than 30 rounds into the crowd, striking eight students aged 15 to 17. One 16-year-old was shot nine times, according to the Philadelphia Inquirer. The article said that police recovered from one suspect's home "a .40-caliber Glock 22 pistol with an extended magazine, laser pointer, and a 'switch,' a small device that attaches to a semiautomatic gun and makes it capable of fully automatic fire."

No motive has been publicly announced, but the police commissioner suggested the attack might be related to a shooting two days earlier at another high school not far from our home. We continue to travel the circuit from our place to Andre's without fear of gun fire, and yet teenagers and their parents in the city rightly worry as kids go to and from school each day.

Diameter

Moon reflects on afternoon pond
too hot for February, orange carp
lurk in the stones below a steady
flow over rock wall. I step away

from our conversation even when
your words concern me most. Clouds
all wrong, lavender croci spring up
two weeks early & crows complain

above us, their eyes on the hawk
they're ready to berate. Slam &
stink never far from us no matter
how the photo frames the circus

scene: ringmaster shoots, strong
man, acrobat, unkempt lion scatter
leaving only scuffs in the sawdust
ring, the meager audience mute.

Circumference

Neither inside nor outside perimeter, limit
border or edge; osmotic wall, semi-permeable
membrane; ethnic, psychic divide; brick
& razor wire, broken glass on cinder block;

In you look out, out you look in

checkpoint, ticket booth, toll lane, passport
stanchions' retractable belt; court metal detector
hinged patio French, panic room outswing
level II doors; Berlin, Hadrian, Tenochtitlan

In you breathe out, out you breathe in

Ming Great Wall; police barricade, OSHA
pennants, Tundra flagging tape, wire back
orange silt fence; Ouroboros, Conestoga
wagons ring colonials, DC Transit busses

In you swim out, out you swim in

seal off the White House; iris recognition
voice activation, Norton antivirus anti-
malware; blood-brain barrier, mind / word
mind / thing; from mouth to anus, toilet to

In you stretch out, out you stretch in

sewer; road rage curse, sweet love
nothings; warn toddler, signal turn,
heel dog, salute guard; fire lookout
tower, laser curtain, flood sluice gates.

In you yearn out, out you yearn in

Stir the Pot

On a raw March day my mother might simmer a split pea soup on the stove all afternoon. In those years we were stationed in Landstuhl Army Medical Center &, before my father died, Mom was at home every day when I came back from school. She would have me pull up a chair & stir the pot to be sure the thick soup didn't burn on the bottom.

Soviets built the Wall just before we arrived in Germany, and my father wanted us all to see how they had divided East from West. Our family took a trip to Berlin to visit Checkpoint Charlie, the place where a few people on official business could cross the border. Dad went over to the East by military bus & came back to report to us in such detail that many years later I thought I'd been on the tour with him.

Mom would cut a few kosher hot dogs into the pea soup for flavor. My brother & I would each get two or three red round fat slices in our bowls at dinner. If our father was home from work, he might tell us about his latest patient—a GI who got his cheek bitten off in a barroom fight, a baby born with a cleft lip & palette, a general with a burn scar that healed badly—or he would quiz me on my times tables, which of course I hated. Sometimes I would tell him about my latest invention, & he would explain why it wouldn't work.

Center

> *exactly resembling, exactly in resemblance exactly*
> *and resemblance. For this is so. Because.*
>
> Gertrude Stein

Let's keep it simple. Stand wherever
you choose & slowly turn your head,
casting your eyes in every direction.

Rain falls on sheds & withered trees
torched cars, a steeple tipping in wind,
bomb craters, shrapnel scarred

trolleys on their sides, furious storm
sweeping mud off hills to the sea.
Stillness. The sound engineer cut off

all ambient noise—his family hasn't
eaten in weeks—while the director fumes
that nobody would buy this script: too

much realism, too childish the notions of
justice & divine retribution. Speech runs
out long before the conflict ends. Actors

go home shaking their heads, blaming
bleak humor, unbelievable characters
a tortured plot wrapped in graveyard

reveries & preposterous battles leaving
bodies in the rubble, a tragedy staged
for the cold camera & a dazed public.

One weekend, cousins we hadn't seen in years came to visit us. Soon after they arrived, the oldest of the three had to go to the emergency room because his breathing tube—which had been sustaining him for two years since he'd gotten out of the hospital after months because of covid—had become blocked and needed attention. While our cousin was recovering the next day, my brother developed severe chest pains and breathing problems of his own. In the ER, the doctor said to him: "Good news. You aren't having a heart attack. But it's likely you have advanced lung cancer."

"I wish I would never have made this film," said the Oscar winner. He preferred instead a world where Russia had not invaded his country and killed tens of thousands of people. What shall we say about the films that tell of the Holocaust in Europe, the Nakba disaster in Palestine, the building of the Israeli state, the occupation of Gaza and West Bank, the shameless Hamas attack on Israelis, the massive reprisals against Gaza—how shall we film all those deaths over all those years?

Area

Perhaps we'd better
          not speak of this. Tea mugs
half finished, we see outside
          rain darkens our neighbor's
driveway, a kid's toy
          gun soaked beside a half-
pumped basketball on
          grass—to these nouns
normal happenings attach—
          a child comes out to play

but cancer, massacre
          invasion, famine find
a home in lists, statistics
          & technical terms.
Their verbs elude us
          or lead down halls
into deserts that flower
          after storm drops
thick tears on bleached
          dirt below thunder

unheralded by light. I
          always thought poets
could name proscribed
          areas reserved for eyeless
reptiles & flightless birds
          tracking on sand by sea

where coral won't grow
        & fish feed on algal bloom
like cattle on rotted
        hay. I could be wrong.

Ordinary Hymns

Attention

A dream had me applying for jobs to stay
in Silver Spring, my high school town. Funny
to watch yearning & confused pain float down
Sligo Creek where, years ago, cicada screamed
from grasses & wet logs. Perhaps my wife's
recent woodcut returned me to that place: her
procession of medieval fools & fate spinners
animal eyes peering from shells & hollows
a fox skeleton shadowing market vendors.
When I was in school, time lingered, more

encumbered by worry but less etched in faces.
Days & weeks pass now without stopping, no
thought slows the parade. Dinners planned with
friends approach, occur & flow away, water over
stones. Indeed, another muddle. Once I neither
knew the origin of streams nor cared where
creeks emptied into distant seas. Today I strain
to keep attention on leaves & twigs the current
sweeps by while mind strays ahead or behind
as if knowing could make the moment stay.

In this heat

I found six cherry stones beside the compost jar
on the kitchen counter this morning. Not spared
to fabricate headache medicine or homemade
adornment nor to fill sacks warmed in the oven
for neck pain, the stones must've spilled out
last night when I cleaned up after dinner. My
aim obviously isn't true, especially when I hurry
so we can watch our evening show. A high
pressure system's forming over our region
tomorrow, sealing in unseasonable temperatures
for the next week like foil over a baked casserole.
August flowers are blooming these June days &
formerly magnificent sycamores die slowly on

our street from some disease or graceless old
age. Our grandson hears barking & wants
to find the source, but the neighbors (two
doctors moved in a few years ago but never
seem home) have locked their Bernese Mountain
Dogs behind a high wooden fence. I dreamed
my parents—not my real parents—stole
from a fund I managed for dispossessed
youth. A song played over & over in my
sleep but when I woke I couldn't recall the
lyrics or follow the beat. Will worms reduce
cherry stones to black humus that can feed
tomatoes & sweet peppers in this heat?

Covenant

Light rain fell outside while my face
in the mirror became everyone I had
ever met or would meet, my now in
covenant with many thens. An empty
ark cast off into choppy water. I couldn't

remember my times tables or wrongs
done me on playgrounds & school rooms.
Flood covered blacktops & parked cars,
teachers on upper floors called to pupils
lost below. A fox screamed in the street.

Later I was a vole on a wooded hill
drowning in the downpour. Still later
a red-winged blackbird, I flew thru
low dark clouds over seas & mountain
tops looking for a branch to rest on.

Heat followed cold, south followed north
waves receded but winds blew without
apology or regret. Fire without war, hunger
without famine, hands & feet without
bodies, vines binding the stoutest trees.

Bookcase

I moved a bookcase today, translating
books that had settled there to a place
on the floor, stowing them in outlandish
order side by side until the shelves were

empty & ready to be dusted. I found a
mess of dust behind the volumes—ones
I'd read & studied, ones I hadn't opened
since I brought them home--& then I

simply had a bit of furniture to drag across
the wooden floor into a vacant space. The
books assumed a new demeanor, joined by
those displaced from other shelves. Now

they sit, not quite configured to great effect
nor resistant to their new roles as protector,
detractor, ticket taker, warden. I consider
every day giving them to others who still

believe in them, but every day I look to them
for strength they can't confer. Books neither
stop death nor recover beauty. While they
collect dust, at best they burn away illusion.

Bandstand

A rare, exasperating form of tinnitus
where you hear music
Mike Kitay

I could call a long black car to pick us up & take us
across the bridge—water below reflecting stone
arches—& geese, not yet gone for the winter, search the reeds
near the bank for food or follow little children in hopes
of breadcrumbs or potato chips. Our friends would
send on our belongings before neighbors realize we'd
vanished. Decades of war effort or preparation for battles
that may never be fought, rations that never satisfy our
hunger, silent entreaties that amount to prayer. Sky grows
angry tho snow no longer falls in our latitude, leaves
merely dry on the branches but don't fall. I keep hearing
tinny dance tunes no one else seems to hear, the volume
rises & falls but I can't make the songs fade or change tempo.
Traffic moves to my inner beat, a delivery man hurries
up the sidewalk as horns & drums crescendo, strings hush
before the crash finale. Soon all this will be packed up &
shipped to our new home, a village with a bandstand in a
manicured park near a swift river. A water wheel, no
longer driving a grist mill, turns for the sake of tourists. It'll be
pleasant until someone notices us in the market or café
& we'll have to move again before the bombing starts.

Split Pea Soup

If I want to make split pea soup for dinner,
I open to a stained page in the cookbook
which says in my hand on top: "Not so many
peas/nor so much water." When did I write that?

In what city & for whom was I cooking? Our son
must have been a little boy, my brother healthy
as always, my mother still alive. A squirrel
climbs a tall pine as I skin the garlic, mince

onions & celery. Now Aaron's cancer threatens
to take him away, Leo's got his own son who
runs to him when we drop the little boy home,
my mother's ashes have fed a cherry tree

for over twenty years. I cut carrots & a potato
while the peas simmer in broth with bay leaf
salt & dry mustard, then toss the vegetables
into the pot, leave it on low a few hours

with occasional stirring. I turn my mind
to writing—shut off radio news of turmoil
& cruelty, resist worry over dear ones or
pain in my own back—peas release into

a smooth green thick sea, ready for red
wine vinegar, pepper, sesame oil, parsley.
Aroma fills the kitchen without words
beyond ingredients, chopping, fire, & time.

One path

One path leads to another
paved road, gravel or dirt.
Rain-filled ruts now ice over.

Beyond pines, heavy traffic noise.
A field not mowed since spring
long ago, cabins vacant for

coming winter. A trail into woods
dark but for occasional sun
patches, a final copse bordering

the racetrack fence. Few leaves
still fall, confuse the mind, pain
fills & empties the brain tide.

Sparrows inspect meadow grass
squirrels test dead branches
downy woodpeckers & nuthatches

feed in flocks. Nothing
desperate. No beginning
nor ending to surprise.

Ordinary Hymns

Dancer

Trumpet vines freeze on garden wall
aerial rootlets halt their blind purpose.
Eyes maunder the horizon, drop to dirt
toadstool or puffballs, yellow scum pine

pollen edging the lake shore, crust at
mouth's corner after morning dream.
Etched reflection under arched bridge,
dome written on agate heaven, shrapnel

scar across child's cheek, toy lettuce
leaves dot a winter patch. Truck
screams into revelers, copter circles
festive scene searching for a running

man in blue stocking cap. News
breaks the black screen, burnishes
the snow. I can't write while voices
stir below, till doors shut & house

resumes its basso. Pipes repeat the tune
drums beat. Medieval dancer looks
away, arms crossed, a pigeon on her
shoulder, magpie bragging at her feet.

Grim men arrive

Grim men arrive in deuce & a halves,
green canvas flaps as they jump down
their boots hitting cobblestone still
wet from last night's storm. In bright

day, sparrows dodge away, crows
jeer in bare oaks & sycamore. Soldiers
set up their barricades & checkpoints
to control the crowds that never come.

A few off-duty uniforms sit & smoke
while others guard the empty avenue.
The populace at home watch news,
not venturing out for food or drink.

Night falls & troops light fires in
50-gallon drums. Occupation without
warning or stated purpose brings frost,
tents go up in dark yards & parks.

For Young Gil

Baby born on Thursday at 9:33 PM
with wait, pain, haste & finally joy.
Mother holds the boy, then father can.
Grandmother will get her turn. Others

around the world wish to hold him too.
Time starts again. He prevents neither
war nor infamy, but troops couldn't stop
him entering here. Don't sign a truce or

cement an alliance in his name. Construct
him no cities. He rolls the moon in his sleep
gathers sea waves & alters the earth's tilt
simply by feeding at his mother's breast.

Thousands of miles away, my room
grows warmer. Wind outside bends
apple branches & a cardinal pair search
our yard for a thicket to build their nest.

His grandfather wanted to see this day.
When the boy is older, perhaps I'll read
him impossible poems his mother's father
made & sing songs my friend left behind.

A tick crawls

A tick crawls across my broadcloth
wandering in blue folds as a thought
might make its way past bus stops
bakeries, shoe shops, a hat emporium

dodging sunlight in favor of cracks in
red & brown brick, searching for a spot
to burrow down, hold fast. Ticks like
memory draw blood; geese return to

the creek they left last fall. No clock
measures their hour. Exactly as you
might have drawn the map at home
the path turns toward a pine grove.

I take one step & then another, inch
toward a bench in shade where I rest
& contemplate what I've done, what I've
lost. A great idleness, chattering of jays.

That rascal

That rascal stares from shattered walls
embers cast darkness, sirens trumpet
a jazz hush across the pocked street.
One more block in any direction, one

more chain link fence, certainty vanishes
like spring ephemerals. When we arrive,
I always said, someone'll know exactly
whom to greet & whom to snub, but no luck

follows me past rowhomes & that rascal leers
from broken porches. Hurrying home in case
a package comes or poppies open in the unkempt
yard, I accept that no one cares despite much press:

the sudden rush to toss compost & sweep away
yesterday's debris ushers in tomorrow's hubris.
Disappointing, & yet what did I expect on a shoe-
string budget & no time to memorize my lines?

Hunger itself

Hunger itself serves no useful purpose.
Garden soil holds the rain in pools beneath
zucchini flowers, green tomatoes, string
beans curling into form. We drink mint tea

& look outside: the weed pile soaked in
sudden storm, next door brick walls &
roof shingles darken in early twilight,
hollyhocks bent pink to the pavement by

unpredicted wind that ripped at larkspur
purple clusters but left low marigolds'
yellow undisturbed. The fox who comes
around seems to eat what little treated food

we leave, but will medicine cure her mange
or boiled eggs satisfy her hunger? Red trucks
rush to a fire; flooded streets & downed
pines mock their shrieking self-importance.

Following wind

Following wind across the path to a stony site
where they honor the family that once owned
this woods, I see traces of orange the sun
hasn't cleared from the horizon, mist clings

to rocks & saplings despite warblers' spell
or raves from jagged jays. I seem to go in
no direction, willingness to leave my bed
won't overcome my desire to stay asleep.

All judgement left at home, my simple
nature expects to see ghosts rip night's fabric.
The sheen on tin pond shivers as frogs burrow
themselves in green-flecked mud till shadows

cast by hand-laid stones in cool morning dusk
conjure cities where young men are bound & shot
while I breathe in my sleep. You say: don't go
back into that room. I try to follow your advice.

Obsidian

This bit of obsidian I found along a river
tiny shard not longer than my fingernail
chipped from a mountain wearing down a
thousand ages beyond sunset, smaller

than any creature I've glimpsed since
opening my eyes. Bullets fired in confusion
mine exploded underfoot long after treaties
banned them, house slumped when blocks

give way to water, cardinal chick falls from
the nest & starves in dirt beside a bike path.
One raving man lifts his mother's bones,
another lies stunned on playground pavement:

fathers & sons drive limos & hearses, contracts
& bonds, wills & deals. From obsidian grows
godhead wider than graveyard, higher than
rain in drought or trust among demons.

Dry sycamore bark cracks beneath my boots
a hot first day of autumn. Somebody's blood
spattered between railroad ties, even now trains
running in the wrong direction stop on time.

About Eli Goldblatt

Eli Goldblatt was born in Cleveland, Ohio, and grew up on Army posts in the U.S. and Germany before attending high school in Silver Spring, Maryland. After earning his B.A. at Cornell University, he attended a year of medical school, traveled in Mexico and Central America, and taught high school for 6 years in Philadelphia. He completed a Ph.D. in English at the University of Wisconsin-Madison in 1990.

His poems have appeared since 1972 in small literary journals such as *Epoch*, *Hambone*, *The Pinch*, *Hubbub*, and *Cincinnati Review*. He is Professor Emeritus of English at Temple University, where he directed writing programs and an institute focused on community-related literacy projects in North Philadelphia, New City Writing. He walks regularly in Wissahickon Creek Park with his wife, artist Wendy Osterweil.

Other Books by Eli Goldblatt

Poetry

Wissahickon Creek: Walks & Dreams (chapbook)

For Instance

Without a Trace

Speech Acts

Sessions 1-62

Journeyman's Song (chapbook)

Herakles: A Verse Play

Composition and Literacy Studies

Alone with Each Other: Literacy and Literature Intertwined

Literacy as Conversation: Learning Networks in Urban and Rural Communities. (Written with David Jolliffe)

Writing Home: A Literacy Autobiography

Because We Live Here: Sponsoring Literacy beyond the College Curriculum

`Round My Way: Authority and Double-Consciousness in Three Urban High School Writers

Children's Books

Lissa and the Moon's Sheep

Leo Loves Round

About Chax

Founded in 1984 in Tucson, Arizona, Chax has published more than 250 books in a variety of formats, including hand printed letterpress books and chapbooks, hybrid chapbooks, book arts editions, one-of-a-kind books, and trade paperback editions such as the book you are holding.

Chax stands against all attacks on democracy, civil rights, and the dignity and self-determination of all peoples, in the USA and internationally. We stand against authoritarian government, including that which exists within supposedly democratic systems. We stand against all racism, bigotry, and misogyny, and against all genocides, including the one being enacted presently in Gaza against the Palestinian people. We stand for equal human rights for all, and we encourage and believe in peace and love as critical to solving problems in our world.

Your support of our projects as a reader, and as a benefactor, is much appreciated.

Our current mailing address is 6181 East 4th Street, Tucson, Arizona 85711-1613 / USA.

You can email us at *chaxpress@chax.org*.
Find CHAX online at *https://chax.org*.

From Away has been designed by Charles Alexander. The image on the cover is *Hiker*, mixed media collage by Wendy Osterweil. This first edition is printed by KC Book Manufacturing.